UNLOCKING THE 7

SECRET POWERS
OF THE HEART

A Practical Guide to Living
in Trust and Love

Shai Tubali

EARTHDANCER

AN INNER TRADITIONS IMPRINT

First edition 2018

Shai Tubali
Unlocking the 7 Secret Powers of the Heart
A Practical Guide to Living in Trust and Love

This English edition © 2018 Earthdancer GmbH
Editing by JMS books LLP (www.jmseditorial.com)

Cover design: DesignIsIdentity.com
Cover illustration: LaFifa (background),
 Gorbash Varvara (heart), both shutterstock.com
Typesetting: DesignIsIdentity.com
Typeset in Minion and Myriad
Printed and bound in China by Midas Printing Ltd.

ISBN 978-1-62055-812-6 (print)
ISBN 978-1-62055-813-3 (e-book)

Published by Earthdancer, an imprint of Inner Traditions
www.earthdancerbooks.com, www.innertraditions.com

MIX
Paper from
responsible sources
FSC® C137129

Contents

Introduction: Meet Your Heart

The myth of the fragile heart

At first glance, the title of this book might seem rather contradictory. Heart and powers? Generally, the word "power" makes us think of energies such as ambition, control, discipline, determination, and stamina. It seems odd, and even somewhat unreasonable, to associate power with love, tenderness, and vulnerability. When we look within ourselves for sources of power and qualities such as fearlessness and resilience, our heart is not the first or most immediate place that comes to mind. Indeed, the mind—the seat of our mental and logical reasoning—tells us that relying on the heart's energies might make us weaker, unable to cope, and far too delicate to resist pressures and protect ourselves. We would end up utterly fragile in a violent and unrestrained world and vulnerable to abuse or exploitation.

But is it true? This small book carries a strong message: the heart *is* your greatest source of power. In fact, when you search for a sense of self-worth, confidence, and determination in your so-called "tough" areas of willpower and ambition, you lose touch with the one resource that could provide you with immense fortitude. All the qualities and strengths we associate with individual power exist in abundance within your heart.

You probably found this book after being guided by *intuition*— the heart's capacity to recognize in a nonmental and nonlogical way what is true and what is not true. This intuition has gradually moved you away from the conventional sources of individual power: uncompromising ambition and competitiveness, coercion, discipline, and desire. However, renouncing the usual energies of power does not mean you should turn to the other extreme of weakness.

Instead, you can tap into a lesser known power resource that always feels "right." Indirectly, almost all human beings recognize to some extent the power of the heart. Books and films in our popular culture are packed with inspiring stories and mythologies of what people were capable of doing in the name of love and the infinite energies that could motivate men and women when they believed in something with all their heart.

This type of power is literally right under your nose. Though your mind does not trust it, it can confidently and successfully replace the mind as a source of power and, when followed all the way, it proves much more resilient and unshakable. The mind's main strategy is that in order to feel strong, you should toughen your heart, pick up your spear, shield, and helmet, and go out into battle with the world. It guides you to be cautious, but it guides you in this way only because it knows very little of the heart, its true essence, functions, and capacities.

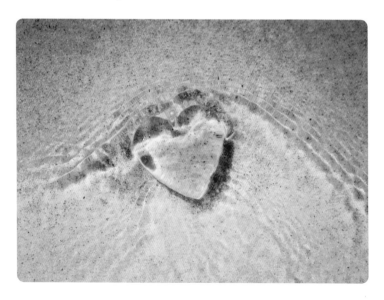

What is the heart?

The way our Western culture approaches the heart is surprisingly dual in nature and contradictory. On the one hand, the general scientific and rational view perceives the heart as a mere physical organ. Indeed, while it is evident that our physical heart contains a complex intrinsic nervous system comprising multiple ganglia (clusters of neurons) that network with each other, we have no accepted indication that this enables the heart to have a "mind" of its own [1]. On the other hand, all cultures throughout human history, including our science-oriented one, have numerous references to the heart as an active element within us that triggers a huge range of states of consciousness, emotions, traits, and expressions. The heart seems to star in our idioms: novels, TV shows, and pop songs alike present characters who express their heart's longings and disappointments. More importantly, whether we consider ourselves "rational" or "emotional," we all know, through our direct experience, what it *feels* like to have our heart "broken."

A mere metaphor? If true, it is definitely a most persistent one. However, if we "listen to our heart," deep down, beneath the layers of skepticism and rationalism, we know it exists.

The heart is where the core or the center of your being—your "innermost"—dwells. When you know your heart, you know your innermost. When your heart is "closed," you are out of touch with your core, or you do not allow others to get to know it. Intuitively, we all recognize that; after all, this *is* the heart's literal meaning. That's why when you "get to the heart of the matter," you have tapped into its central or essential issue. As our innermost, the heart is the deepest place from which we choose and act. It is the center that defines our values and sense of meaning in life. We admire famous figures for heroically "following their heart," for acting only according to their deepest calling despite everything they have been told. Clearly, the heart is associated with our authenticity, our capacity to listen to the voice of our true self, just as yet another common phrase advises us to do—to "listen to our heart." We recognize that the heart is wise. It has its own intelligence, which it speaks in its own language. It is a source of wisdom that connects us directly with what is true in us. For this reason, if there is an internal realm that could serve as the abode of our "soul," it is without doubt our heart.

Even though our mind clearly has many vital functions, it is in this sense only the heart's servant. When we appoint the mind master of our being, we become confused, perplexed, and tense. Trying to "use your head," as many suggest we do when in states of confusion, often leads to a deeper inner turmoil. In the absence of the heart as the one true master of our inner world, the mind loses its balance. You ask it to do things it cannot do. For example, your mind has no idea what the meaning of your life is. Interestingly, neither has the heart any "idea." "Knowing" for the heart is not like knowing how to prepare financial reports, or how to compose an argument in a convincing manner—its "knowing" is more like "feeling." It feels what really matters in life because it is connected to life's deeper sense. Through this feeling it orients itself in important choices and decisions.

Your heart is a source of many vital qualities that the mind could never cultivate: humbleness and courage, intimacy and goodness, acceptance and appreciation, faith and generosity, purity and devotion, compassion and sacrifice. When the heart gets in touch with expressions of such qualities, it awakens our dormant innermost and even moves us to tears. Only the heart can appreciate these qualities. It finds in them extraordinary beauty and value, whereas for the mind they are irrelevant and useless. In addition to its function as the center of our meaning, knowing, and choosing, the heart is of course our emotional center, through which we come into contact with and relate to ourselves and others. Emotions are the heart's tool of communication and through them it weaves "relationships," the flow of give-and-receive between ourselves and the world around us.

By guiding our being toward its core meaning and knowing, our heart is where we choose to whom and to what we should devote our attention, dedication, and passion. This is the deeper meaning of "setting your heart on something." When we devote our fullest attention—when we dedicate ourselves from the innermost "with all our heart"—we are filled with a profound sense of meaning. In Hebrew, "attention" is literally translated as "putting your heart into something"— a clue to the fact that wherever your heart is, this is also where your actual reality is found.

Exercise: Getting to know your heart

For the best results, write down your answers.

Identify a moment or an event in your life in which you felt connected to your heart. Let the memory of that moment or event become alive in you. Immersed in this relived memory, ask yourself: Why do I consider this as being connected to the heart? What does this connection mean to me?

Now identify a moment or event in your life in which you felt your heart was open. Once again, let the memory of that moment or event become alive in you. Then identify a moment or event in which you felt your heart was closed. Recall that moment or event as intensely as possible. Immersed in these two re-awakened memories, ask yourself: What does the heart being open mean to me? What does the heart being closed mean to me?

Heart is power

The purpose of this book is to encourage you to make your heart the center of your being and identity. If you follow its guidance all the way, it can turn your heart into the ultimate reliable inner resource from which you can act with confidence in the world. At the end of this journey, you will see the heart as the one true driver of your life, a supremely active engine that provides all your actions with an inexhaustible reservoir of energy. The way to gain the trust required to make such a crucial move in your life is by recognizing the heart's powers. The reason our mind is capable of convincing us that the heart is a hazardous place in which to be lies in its argument that the heart is fragile. But as you awaken more and more fully these seven previously unknown and unused powers of your heart, you will transcend all doubt and fear.

Notice that I use the term "awaken" rather than "develop" or "achieve." Once again, the heart has a language of its own: with the heart, you never learn something you have not known; rather, a dormant memory in you awakes and becomes activated.

Although there are more secret heart powers, the following seven powers have been selected carefully and are the most essential in taking a first step toward a full activation of your heart and love:

Heart wisdom—revealed through your heart's knowing beyond doubt. You no longer need to pretend that you are confident.

Strength in vulnerability—surprisingly, achieved through openness, being vulnerable, and unconditional love. You do not need to toughen up to shield yourself from the world.

Freedom through forgiveness—gained through the magic of forgiveness. You do not need to keep on fighting old ghosts to prove you were right.

The ability to love—discovered through your heart's natural abundance, even when the mind tells you that you have nothing to give. You do not require endless processes of self-improvement and healing to become a giver.

Emotional transformation—the ability to transform any internal energy (anxiety, desire, or frustration) by simply placing yourself in your heart. You do not need to become entangled in emotions and feelings that lead you nowhere when you have such a powerful transformer inside.

Empowerment without limits—awakened as you get to know your heart as life's engine. You no longer need to rely on willpower and ambition, which involve anger, competition, and stress.

Loving yourself—established as you connect more and more with your heart's essential contentment. You do not need to wait until you are worthy enough or until someone else is ready to give you this recognition.

May the knowledge of these seven heart powers lead you to activate your heart wisely in accordance with its original destiny and purpose!

Basic Heart Activation

Practiced daily, this basic activation exercise enables you to gradually shift the center of your being to your heart. The ideal is to start your day with it, but you can do it at any other time, including just before going to sleep.

To avoid your mind intruding during the exercise, allow yourself to follow the guidance in an effortless and gentle way, without trying to do it "perfectly." It is the general response of your being to this ongoing activation that really matters.

To begin with, follow the activation while reading the instructions. After a few times, when you feel confident enough, you can activate your heart with closed eyes.

Position

Sit comfortably, but do not slouch. Keep your chest wide open, not rigidly but in a relaxed manner. It is important not to close or lock the chest; people often tend to let their shoulders lean too far forward. Instead, allow the shoulders to fall gently backward, so that you can feel your entire chest area open and spacious, as if you were presenting it to the world. You may feel that widening the chest releases a new energy stream, which might even flow upward to the throat area. This is both perfectly natural and welcome. Make sure your fingers remain loose and that the palms of your hands are open, so that you give and receive in an endless flow of interaction.

Step one: Sink into your chest

Take a deep breath and then breathe slowly and deeply, relaxing your body with every breath you take. In this activation, you will learn how to sink into the chest area. This shift of your awareness, being, and identity to the chest should be physical, not just metaphorical. We are used to having the center of our being in the head area. This makes sense: our eyes, ears, mouth, and brain are located there, which means that the head is the place from which we look, hear, speak, and perceive. On the other hand, feel how overloaded this area is, unnaturally full of overthinking and overjudging. This is the result of being *too* oriented in the head.

With the help of breathing, visualizing, intention, and feeling, feel how you are slowly and gently sinking with your very sense of "I" into the chest area. It is as if you are actually moving all the overactive energy in the head to the chest. Breathe gently into the chest area while feeling more and more that this is where "you" are.

From your new location in the chest, the brain, eyes, ears, and mouth are mere tools rather than who you are. You can always use your head, but you are not your head. Feel how you place your sense of "I am" in the chest, deciding that this is where you are going to meet everything in your life. It is from the chest that you will look at and respond to everything.

Try to feel how your central vision—like a pair of hidden eyes—is located in the chest area. Through these eyes alone you actually look at the world inside you and outside you.

Imagine that you have "lost" your head—as if instead of your physical head there is now a pure space. Feel as if your "head," your headquarters, has moved to your chest. This is not only where you look from, but also where you hear and talk. What happens when you look out from here at everything? What are the qualities of vision and listening that belong to this area and that are different from your usual sight and hearing? Does this shift to the chest relax anything? Does it make your vision more sweet, compassionate, and forgiving?

Try to look at a particular challenge or conflict in your current life from your new "head." How do you see this issue in your life from the perspective of your heart? How do you perceive others—perhaps those who are a part of your conflict—from this space? How do you see your life in general? Breathe into your new center of perception. With every breath, feel how the chest expands at the expense of the head area and opens up even more. It is not a shy area to conceal and protect, it is your proudest center. How wide can you open it up? The wider it gets, the more the head area is "consumed" by it, relaxing into its new position as a servant of your heart.

Step two: Turn your heart outward

Let go of the thought that awakening this center should be a lengthy process. Simply do it now. Ordinarily, all the energy in the chest area turns inward in a mechanism of self-defense and self-absorption. Instead, supported by the wide-open posture of your chest, gently change the direction of the energy and feel how your chest is opening up toward the world. It unfurls and spreads like a fully open flower. It is not going to hide and rest within itself. It will not keep its energy to itself but instead is available for communication, completely released, its gaze now turned to the world.

Recognize that since this is where your true self abides, this is the place from which "you" come forward to greet the whole world. Feel what relief this new position brings, with the chest facing the world instead of collapsing into itself. With every breath, let it gently open up and come out even more. Do not think of the consequences or withhold because of emotional reactions. Simply play with it energetically and allow it to happen physically.

Step three: Declare your heart's intention

Make it your clear intention to remain like this even after the completion of the activation. This activation is your readiness to come out to the world, saying "yes" to your life from your innermost. The energetic expression of saying "yes" from your innermost is sinking into your chest and opening it up from there like a flower. This immediately removes all subtle resistance and protective mechanisms and, at the same time, relaxes the overworked and ineffective mental machine. In its role as your new head, what does your heart know today? Is there anything, even just one single thing, that it knows deeply and beyond any doubt? Declare this knowing to yourself.

Finally, take one more deep breath into the chest, and slowly and gradually come out of the meditation. As you gently open your eyes, retain the sense of an open chest and outward flow.

You might feel that sometimes your mind resists allowing the sinking and opening to take place. It might try to convince you that "this isn't the right time to open up so much," or ask "what's the point of doing this every day?" Remember, the mind is like a king struggling for his dominion. Who would give away their kingdom so readily? Make sure your activation exercise does not turn into a battle with the mind. Since one of the heart's powers is its ability to be all-containing, it never really needs to fight. Simply relax and place yourself where you are most reasonably meant to be.

Practicing this activation exercise daily will eventually allow it to become a natural energetic impulse. At first, your heart will tend to resume its habitual position and direction, and your mind will quickly take over your being once more. With time, however, this exercise will make residing in your brain as your "home" feel very unnatural. You will feel the over-activity in your head reducing in intensity, and order in your kingdom will be established; the false king will become an effective servant once again and the rightful king will fulfill its birthright.

You can activate your heart at any given moment, including when you are not practicing the exercise. When you regard something, whether internally or externally, or when you need to make a decision, whether great or small, remember to first let your being sink into your chest, dissolving the thinking mind with all its contradictions, and see what happens when you look at it from your new center. Another way to allow the heart's magic to take effect swiftly in your daily

life is by pushing the energy from the center of the chest outward more and more. Your emotional and mental states will
soon follow this shift in direction.

First Secret: Heart Wisdom

Your heart always knows what your mind forgets

Our brain is very often overcrowded with doubts and mistrust. We start to feel lost and confused, no longer sure of what is right and what is wrong. We hope so much that we will develop confidence in our mind and yet doubt always creeps in. But what can be done? How can we achieve any sense of knowing in such states, with so many contradictory thoughts running around in our mind? Before answering this question, we need to understand a few things about our mind and the nature of thinking.

The mind is *by its very nature* contradictory. As ironic as it may sound, it is never "single-minded." Any thought in one direction is accompanied by a thought in the other direction, any opinion by its opposite opinion, and anything can be looked at from another perspective. It is not only in arguments and debates that we sometimes have an entirely legitimate opposing view; it happens constantly within our mind, where our thoughts convince us—and unconvince us—very efficiently on almost any matter or subject.

Add to this the fact that our mind is quite exposed to *external pressures*. Again, this is its nature: the mind absorbs influences easily, which is why it can become conditioned so quickly. Perhaps you are still struggling to release your mind from childhood conditioning, social morality, and expectation.

One last characteristic of the mind is that it is not meant to tell you what is true or real. Its role is learning and registering *how* life functions. Since it is all about functionality, you can confidently consult your mind when you need to remember how to drive your car or work out your schedule. Try, on the other hand, to seek its advice about things that really matter—such as your life's meaning, purpose, and true path—and your mind will be utterly confused. Under such unnatural pressure, it will simply show you all the possible "pros and cons," to the point where you become even more torn and divided inside. Everything will seem reasonable and, at the same time, nothing will.

Of course, none of us can eliminate doubt or confusion completely, nor should we aspire to achieve such a perfect doubt-free state. Sometimes it is essential to go through "crises" of uncertainty in order to transcend a situation and make the leap to the next phase. However, even then, in our darkest moments, it is important to have an anchor of a solid, unbreakable knowing, or we might sink into sheer hopelessness. And it is not the mind that will offer us a real solution. The mind is very good at presenting problems, not at revealing crystal-clear, insightful solutions. The bottom line is that if you are seeking heart wisdom, seek it in the correct part of your being.

*

This is where the first secret power of the heart comes in: your heart always *knows* what your mind forgets. I call the heart the "body of knowing." It is the center in you that knows the truth, even when your body trembles with anxiety, your mental center is crammed with negative thoughts, and your emotional center is in a state of overwhelming turmoil. "Knowing" is remarkably different from "thinking." While thinking always offers concepts and possibilities in contradictory pairs, knowing cannot be contrasted with some thought or other. It exists beneath all fluctuating thoughts. Unlike feelings, emotions, and thoughts, it does not obey the law of constant change. It is, in essence, permanent and eternal. Our thinking tells us there is no such thing, except perhaps for some repeatedly proven laws of science. Yet knowing that you can know without a shadow of doubt is a power beyond the realm of thinking. Of course, your knowing could evolve and expand, and be redefined more deeply or accurately. Yet, fundamentally, it is indestructible. It is what our innermost recognizes as "true." In contrast to knowledge, which tells us how things work, knowing is direct: it is a feeling and an insight into the nature of things. It is ungraspable by linear and logical thinking, almost like a subtle, silent smile within your heart.

Unlike what we may *think*, our heart accumulates a great deal of knowing throughout life. This knowing is sometimes the "nectar" we extract from the flowers of our different experiences. Indeed, the wisdom that we carry with us from our deepest life experiences is not affected by fleeting thoughts. However, an even greater part of our knowing is simply here, within our heart, regardless of what we know from experience during our lifetime.

This is the mysterious connection between knowing and remembering. While knowledge is seen as something you acquire and add to your understanding, knowing feels much more like a reawakened memory—something you have always somehow known, yet your mind has forgotten.

There are clear indications of this reawakening of dormant memory. When you know instantly that something is true, your body recognizes it physically and a profound inner "Yes!" seems to emerge from your very cells, which your body experiences physically. Sometimes we are filled with tears—beautiful, happy tears that come directly from within our heart in response to deeper truths.

One of my all-time favorite stories that bears such deeper truths is the Buddhist legend of the Chinese Bodhisattva Quan Yin entering heaven [2].

As soon as the great saint leaves her body, her soul is elevated toward the golden gates of heaven. Both just outside and beyond the gates a holy crowd of saints, masters, and angels awaits her, full of admiration for the legacy of illumination the "Goddess of Mercy" has been able to leave behind her on Earth. Quan Yin is just one step from passing through the gates, but something bothers her. She looks down below her feet and sees planet Earth full of misery and confusion. Utterly lost sentient beings scream for guidance. She then asks the other great beings: "But what will happen to all those suffering beings?" and they answer: "Oh, do not worry about them! You did your share. They will require many incarnations and a great deal of learning through suffering to attain Buddhahood. This could take many thousands of years, although a relatively short time in cosmic terms. Eventually, one day, they will all join us in enlightenment." Quan Yin listens to their answer attentively and then looks again beneath her feet. Intellectually, she understands the answer very well, yet her heart refuses to follow. She tells her fellow masters: "You are asking me to enter the gate, but how can I leave a part of my body outside? The enlightenment that has been revealed to me was the truth of oneness. All these beings below are my legs and hands. How could I possibly enter without a leg or a hand? I can only enter as a complete being and a full body. I will therefore never enter the gate, until all sentient beings will be able to follow. We shall enter as one." True to her word, the Bodhisattva has never taken that one step into heaven and she remains there forever, waiting.

Whenever I tell this story—which inspires many in the Buddhist Mahayana tradition to take the known "Bodhisattva Vow"—in a lecture or a seminar, most of the participants become overwhelmed and tearful. They may not be as mature as the Buddha and able to make such a bold and selfless commitment, but they are instantly reminded of a deeper truth about life's meaning and purpose. They cry because their heart recognizes the truth through the thick veils of their forgetful mind.

Exercise: Recognizing what you know

The following exercise is the easiest way to recognize your heart's capacity to remember and know. Think of an event or moment when you heard, read, watched, or experienced something that touched you deeply and perhaps even brought you to tears. It could be a scene from a movie that made you cry, a lecture or a passage in a book that shook you to the core, or a beautiful moment with people that was so real it moved you uncontrollably. As soon as you have your moment, write down what it was that you responded to so strongly and the way in which you responded (physically, emotionally, energetically, and perhaps spiritually). Ask yourself: "What truth about life's meaning and purpose was my heart reminded of? What knowing did I recognize during that event?" If more than one moment or event came to you, repeating the exercise again and again can only deepen your insight and prepare you for the second exercise of this chapter (The Book of Knowing).

All of us have experienced moments or events that reawakened our heart's memory. Once the intensity of those moments has dissipated, we tend to think, mistakenly, that they were just "experiences" and are now lost. We expect that the experience must return in order for us to know once more. But these were not just experiences. Once your memory is awakened, your body's cells carry it within them. Strangely, we accept that traumas leave unhealthy marks in both the psyche and the body, but when moments are involved in which we come to know the deeper truths of our life, we believe they are wiped away by the strong currents of thought and emotion. The truth is that knowing is far more powerful than the most intense experiences. Every fragment of knowing is like the markings left by the waves of the sea on the shore of your being.

Being overcautious and avoiding defining our understanding and learning as "knowing" is unwise, and yet there is a deeper reason behind this reluctance to fully own our moments of knowing. We are often cautious because we feel that on a social level to know things beyond doubt is to be too arrogant and defiant. However, not knowing does not make us humble, but only more confused and incapable of navigating through the many voices within and without. Knowing is not arrogance. It is actually a kind of silent confidence that nothing can crush, the same feeling that the Beatles captured when singing "Nothing's gonna change my world." Your knowing does not go against society. On the contrary, since it is truly confident, your knowing does does not need to defend or justify itself at all.

To ensure that the body of knowing within your heart is conscious and present at any given moment, you must declare that you know—especially when you need it most, when both your mental and emotional state as well as external circumstances entirely contradict and attack this knowing. This is the deeper meaning of the cliché "to follow your heart." If you follow your heart's knowing persistently, you gradually become far less exposed to pressures. Since knowing is so much more concrete than thoughts, feelings, and experiences, it is your first step to indestructibility. Once you recognize it, you can hold on to it in the face of all destructive emotions and thought patterns. Even in the midst of an anxiety attack, you are still able to reside peacefully within your heart. So listen to your heart and gently answer this question: "What do I know? What do I know with certainty within my heart—a certainty that no doubts can reach or harm?"

To answer this honestly, turn your awareness toward your heart and gradually find there a hidden yet wholly solid conviction. It may not be the kind of conviction that tells you whether to turn right or left on life's path, or exactly what decision you should take at any juncture. But it will certainly tell you what is real for you, even if you have not experienced that enough. Remember that the heart's dormant memory precedes experience.

The first answers might be quite abstract and might mainly concern deeper and general truths about life's meaning and purpose. Since the heart's knowing, unlike the mind's knowledge, is all about the "why" and the "what for"—why we are here; what are the most important values of life—this is a good starting point. Eventually, what you recognize as real will become your heart's compass in more substantial choices and decisions in life.

Exercise: The Book of Knowing

To reveal your body of knowing, create your very own "Book of Knowing." Take a beautiful notebook and start to write down the things you know within the depths of your being, slowly but surely. Take your time. Even if at first you feel satisfied with just one sentence, even a single sentence of knowing that can never be touched by thoughts and emotions is actually a great deal! You can source your knowing from moments and events in which you read, heard, watched, or experienced something so real that it brought you to tears. You can also remind yourself of things that you have always somehow known, for no completely clear reason. A good way of revealing the heart's knowing is to close your eyes, relax, and ask yourself: "If I were an all-knowing teacher, how would I answer my mind's questions?" Now listen carefully and write down everything you "teach" yourself.

Become increasingly aware of the "small" pieces of wisdom you gain from important experiences. In general, this exercise will make you conscious of those moments of recognition in your daily life that you tend to overlook or perhaps may undervalue.

- Do you know that you are a soul and not a mere physical and mortal being?
- Do you know that something exists beyond the senses?
- Do you know that love is an invincible power?
- Do you know that a certain partnership you have is the type that lasts for the rest of your life?
- Do you know that you have a certain mission to complete in this lifetime?
- Do you know that anger is caused by fear?
- Do you know that fulfillment of desire cannot really satisfy your soul?
- Do you know that there is one thought or emotion that you must overcome in this lifetime?

Compile and consolidate your Book of Knowing gradually, as it springs increasingly from your heart. Whenever you are overcome by fear or doubt, read it in order to remind yourself of this silent smile within. Hard times may happen, but with your book at your side, you can remain confident in their midst. Feel how your knowing glows in the dark— indeed, glows more brightly in the dark, as even the smallest sources of light tend to do. Whenever you hold on to your knowing despite your thoughts, emotions, and feelings, this book becomes a reality. A day will come when you will embody this book and become your knowing. This is what can be thought of as a fully embodied soul.

Second Secret:
Strength in Vulnerability
You are unbreakable when you are vulnerable

Your mind cannot tell the difference between "*vulnerable*" and "*breakable*." It thinks it is obvious that if you are vulnerable, you are also breakable. Since this sounds logical enough, your mind chooses the strategy of remaining invulnerable as much as possible. Of course, your mind only wants to protect you, as its main role is to keep you safe in a world full of dangers. It registers moments where you were vulnerable and, as a result, became deeply disappointed, rejected, betrayed, or abandoned. This left you not just with an unbearable pain but also with a profound sense of weakness. We are all afraid of being weak. It is a survival instinct: we must not show that we are powerless and defenseless in a hostile and overpowering environment. To conceal this weakness, we put on armor, a thick layer of protection with which we defend our vulnerable heart. This is why we become hard and sometimes react quickly to insults or criticism with anger, hatred, and vengefulness, and harbor grudges.

Your mind strives to become so strong and impenetrable that you will never be harmed or feel pain. To achieve this impregnable condition, it surrounds the heart with a protective wall. This wall is not just a metaphor—you could easily sense it in your chest as a thick layer separating you from the environment and protecting your fragile true being. This wall is not necessarily such a bad idea. If you have no coping mechanism for intense emotions and profound disappointments, it is perhaps wise to keep a thick protective layer around your heart. However, in light of our knowledge of the powers of the heart, we should reexamine this strategy: Does it really work? Do we actually feel safer when our hearts are closed?

A quick, honest look at our life experience tells us, of course, that this strategy does not work very well. The more we feel threatened and in need of defending and protecting ourselves, the more intensely and deeply we feel our own fragility. In the end, the effort to become invulnerable makes us

more vulnerable. The great irony is that the more we contract our heart, the more we feel it needs additional and even
more sophisticated layers of protection, with the result that,
slowly but surely, we stop feeling pain but scarcely feel anything else. We become cautious and numb, hurting little but
also loving little.

*

Your wise heart offers a different strategy. With this secret
power, you can finally remove the wall: vulnerability is your
key to indestructibility. The heart's wisdom defies the effec-
tiveness of the wall. Historically, walls have never really
worked, which is also true for your internal wall. From the
heart's point of view, it is clear that what we believe makes us
stronger actually makes us weaker. However, *what we believe
makes us weaker actually makes us stronger.*

The mind's strategy is based on resistance. It refuses to open
up because it wants to avoid potential disappointments. It
strives with all its might to minimize the pain of betrayal
and rejection, pushing people away as a result and keeping a
clear distance, since people are able to upset our mind-body
system by failing to be there for us. The heart's strategy is
based on love. It continues to trust and open up even if this
could lead to painful experiences. It agrees to pain, because
it knows that it is better to feel pain than to feel nothing, but
that is because it knows the secret that, as long as it remains
open, even if it bleeds a little, it will not be weakened. In

fact, it gets stronger with each opening up, despite the disappointment and hurt.

In reality, it is your mind's resistance to pain that makes these past experiences so painful, imprinting upon you dark and trenchant conclusions about life and people. When you closed up your heart in response to the pain, it took hold of you. Opening up to breathe into it and to contain it completely in fact has the effect of melting it away, leaving the heart refreshed and intact. This is the excellent "contain and include" heart-practice: when there is no resistance and you choose instead to open up even more widely, you become greater than the situation. Contained within your heart, the situation fades away without leaving an unforgettable impression.

Exercise: Flex your heart

Sit quietly, with your eyes open or closed. Try to open your heart as wide as possible, as if you were flexing a muscle. Visualize how you are opening up the chest unconditionally or without hindrance. What does it feel like? Note that your mind might send you false signals of danger. Since you are not really in danger right now, just quietly ignore the signals.

Now do the exact opposite: Try to close your heart as much as possible. Contract your chest and create a wall to separate yourself from the outside world. This should not be too difficult, since it is what we do instinctively whenever we fear the pain of a potential or actual rejection. How do you feel when you close your heart—physically, emotionally, and mentally? How do you behave and act in the world when your heart is closed?

Now, ask yourself: In which of these two states did I like myself the most? In which of them did I feel healthier and more stable? Realize that opening up your heart is not for the benefit of others. It is primarily for you. This is the state when you love yourself the most. Flex and contract your chest area several more times until you feel confident enough to choose the open state.

Generally speaking, the heart is in one of the following three different kinds of condition:

Mostly closed—this is when our mind decides that we've had enough disappointments and betrayals for one lifetime, and so even with those with whom we are close we make sure our heart remains essentially invulnerable and untouched.

Half open—this is when we open and close our heart, depending on circumstances. We open it up with certain people in a safe environment, but even then, only if they are kind to us. The opening is conditional on circumstances and therefore is fluctuating.

Essentially open—this is not only a condition, but also a statement of being. An essentially open heart never closes the door of trust, faith, and communication, despite all disappointments and betrayals.

The state of being half open is the most common: the heart only opens when the situation is clearly safe. It is the mind that allows you to be vulnerable only when there are good reasons to trust. However, this dependency keeps you weaker: it means that your heart opens and closes in response to each and every stimulation, however negligible. This is a fragile heart, constantly searching for signs of approval and recognition and needing to fear any change of circumstances. For the half-open heart, deep emotions such as love and tenderness are too delicate and can only be expressed in a wholly supportive and nurturing environment. The half-open heart is based on what is probably the greatest myth surrounding the heart: that since it is fragile, it requires a safe environment and cannot handle a difficult or hostile world. When the heart encounters intense situations, it withdraws behind the wall, leaving the mind on the front line to fight and negotiate.

This heart's secret power tells us something completely different: love and compassion are not tender but rather invincible powers of our being that channel tremendous cosmic waves. They do not need a secure environment to be revealed; they can be expressed proudly and openly, even in the most strident and noisy marketplace and in the face of strong opposing forces.

Try this exercise the next time someone offends you or when the next hurt inevitably strikes. Remain with an open heart, just as you do during the heart flexing. You will feel an impulse to contract your heart, but take the decision not to do so. Keep the flow of openness and tenderness, and see what happens as a result. With your heart exposed, work with the unconscious expectation that has caused you pain: that people should never be disappointing. The reality is that not only will people disappoint you every now and then, but that this plays a crucial role in your own heart development. Translate your disappointment into the thought that obviously, this person *should* have offended me, and keep the heart open and flowing.

Open your chest fully to the event. Agree to the pain. Direct love toward the person who caused you pain. You will soon discover that this pain flows through you and is transformed into a greater power of love.

*

Your heart does not need protection, it *is* your best protection. Living life with an open heart is not just less damaging than having to defend it, it is, ironically, the very state in which nothing and no one can hurt you. As the heart lets go of expectations and remains wide open, agreeing to feel unconditionally, a point will come when it no longer feels pain but only love. Since that pain was caused by your own false expectations, you will grow confident enough to keep your heart as an open door that never closes and which constantly allows the natural flow of goodness and compassion from within your heart.

Here we return to the difference between vulnerable and breakable. Vulnerability means fearlessly keeping the door to your heart open. A tender heart that does not try to protect itself and remains open to experience, accepting, loving, and forgiving under all circumstances, is an unbreakable heart. There is nothing that it cannot envelop and contain, no power that it cannot melt away, since it agrees to receive whatever penetrates it. What enemy could defeat such a heart? Even the most powerful assailant becomes helpless, as it tries with all its might to attack, hurt, and ruin. The love of such a heart keeps it unharmed. We can only suffer hurt as long as fear lives within our heart. Aggression and destruction feed on our fear but lose all their power in the face of love. Together, love and the heart's openness form the most formidable power in the world—a power that only increases when we love at those times that it makes no sense to open up at all. We fear being hurt, but what can happen if we are willing to get hurt and commit ourselves to love, even in such circumstances?

Many people consider the life of Jesus a perfect example of the heroism of the heart: the way he lived in this harsh world like the most delicate flower—wide open, exposed, and loving. Do we think that those who crucified him defeated him? No, we know that the heart of Jesus could never be crucified, only his body. You cannot crucify a heart whose last words are "Father, forgive them, for they know not what they do."

Exercise: Removing the wall

In essence, there is no such thing as a closed heart. Your heart has never hardened, it has simply been surrounded by the mind's wall, behind which it remains tender and glowing. This is precisely why your mind closed your heart in the first place: it knows that the heart is always willing, open, and innocent. In reality, your heart is forever a "child." It is time to realize that this childlike quality is your key to indestructibility.

Practice this visualization every day for several weeks.

Feel the wall separating your heart from the rest of the world. Then shift your awareness to the heart behind that wall. Recognize how it has remained tender all this time.

Now imagine that you are removing the wall. Feel your heart in the open, laid bare, without the need for protection. Breathe into this total openness. It may not be easy at first, since this is an unfamiliar state, but feel the deep release; after all, you have missed your heart and your heart has missed you.

Offer your heart, golden and glowing, to the cosmos and to the world. Feel how this gesture of offering actually makes you bigger—bigger than life, and greater than any resentment, whether small or more significant, that you might feel from the outside.

Each day as you practice this exercise, gently remove the mind's protective layers one by one. Teach the mind that its fear of doing so only exposes the heart to more harm. Step forward and declare: "From now on, I leave my heart open and choose to love even in the most difficult conditions." With such a bold declaration, nothing has the power to hurt you.

Third Secret:
Freedom through Forgiveness
Forgiveness is a miracle that sets you free

During World War II, when Eva Mozes Kor was just six years old, she was sent with her twin sister, Miriam, and the rest of her family to the death camp Auschwitz. As twins, the small sisters immediately drew the attention of the notorious doctor Josef Mengele, who performed deadly laboratory experiments on the camp prisoners, and on children and twins in particular. While the rest of her family was killed, the two girls managed to survive. At the age of 82, and having taken

American nationality, Eva Kor has become a renowned educator and author, who inspires many people to activate one of their greatest heart powers: forgiveness. If anyone can teach the act of forgiveness, it has to be this extraordinary woman, who became well known when she approached the 96-year-old "bookkeeper of Auschwitz" in the courtroom, and publicly forgave him while hugging and kissing him.

Indeed, she forgave not only him but the entire membership of the Nazi regime. In a public declaration, she stated: "I, Eva Mozes Kor, a twin who survived Josef Mengele's experiments in Auschwitz 50 years ago, hereby give amnesty to all Nazis who participated directly or indirectly in the murder of my family and millions of others." [3]

Your mind, of course, cannot grasp the logic behind such unconditional forgiveness, which was not accompanied by any demand for remorse in return. It is only your wise heart that can be touched by Kor's courageous act, recognizing not only its beauty but also its sense and value. "I never thought that I would ever forgive anybody," she admitted in an interview. However, as soon as she dared to make this step, "Pain was lifted from my shoulders. I was no longer a victim of Auschwitz. I was no longer a prisoner of my tragic past. I was finally free." She realized that "forgiveness is nothing more and nothing less than an act of self-healing and an act of self-empowerment." Now, she encourages others to do the same, passionately telling her audience: "I want you to know that every single one of you is very powerful. You have the power to forgive. No one can give it to you and no one can take it away." [4]

Eva Mozes Kor has clearly understood two major secrets about forgiveness:

- Forgiveness is an act of power, not weakness.
- Forgiveness is the power that can break the chains that connect you to the past and to your victimizers.

While many people know in their minds that they "should" forgive, in order to achieve the level of illumination and release that Kor achieved they need first to understand what forgiveness really means and its importance beyond being the "right thing to do." As soon as such an understanding is gained, it becomes much easier to forgive wholeheartedly and to transform through this act.

The first step is to understand why forgiveness is power.

For the mind, maintaining a grudge and holding on to feelings of disappointment in another person are an effective self-defense strategy, seeing it as a way to compensate for the pain caused. By remaining angry and unforgiving, the mind believes that it holds a position of power that was perhaps completely lost in past moments of deep hurt. Its main argument is that if you are hurt by someone and then forgive them, you lose twice while the other person wins twice. So your mind tells you that you win when you do not forgive.

However, the mind's strategies are rarely effective. For the most part, the mind achieves exactly the opposite of what it hoped to gain. In reality, remaining unforgiving is not empowering at all. Instead, you are preserving your position as a victim and only become weaker and more eaten up inside. When you fail to forgive, *you* lose twice.

Your heart's wisdom, on the other hand, whispers in your ear that when you have the courage to leave behind any immediate feelings of resentment and open your heart to forgive, you become far bigger than both the hurtful memory and the victimizer. This is why Eva Mozes Kor explains that it is not just an act of self-healing but also one of self-empowerment: forgiving expands your being far beyond the previous limitations of victimhood. With forgiveness, the second secret power of the open heart becomes even clearer: by opening your heart wide enough to forgive, you literally become invincible.

In fact, forgiveness is such an indication of power that its capacity combines profound humanness and otherworldly godliness. The human part of our heart alone is unable to realize that. When we are willing to forgive, we form a direct contact with the godly part of our heart—with a transhuman love and transhuman capacity to include and contain. As Kor reminds us, no one can give us this power or take it away, not even God. It is the divinity in us that is demonstrated through such an act.

*

To support the human part of your heart in letting go of its resentment, you need to understand that at the root of your grudge lies an expectation. For some reason, we harbor the hidden assumption that people should not disappoint, betray, or hurt us. Reality, of course, shows us otherwise: people, it seems, are definitely *meant* to disappoint, betray, or hurt us, at least sometimes. We tend to overlook the fact that for others we too are perceived as the people who disappointed, betrayed, and hurt them. What we experience as a so-called "betrayal" is more often than not someone else's need for self-fulfillment. In most cases, it was not directed against us but instead was simply a choice made in their own interests. Taking a close look at those times when we ourselves have been accused of causing pain could enable us to see the truth in this.

Exercise: Let go of the expectation

Write down a list of ten disappointing experiences in your life involving people and situations. Briefly describe what they did and what exactly disappointed and hurt you. Now create two columns; at the top, head the left column "Things people should never do" and the right "Things people must do sometimes." For example, if you write in the left column "Fathers should never ignore their children," then you should write "Fathers must ignore their children sometimes" in the right column.

The fact is that sometimes people have to do these things; that is the reality of our world. People do not necessarily do things specifically against you, they act out of ignorance, or simply because they are busy pursuing their own interest. Remember, trying to control this reality by resisting it only makes you weaker. With each such statement and its complementary opposite, ask yourself: "What is the reality I must embrace?" and after answering this question, look into your heart and ask: "What happens in my heart when I embrace this reality?"

The second enlightenment experienced by Eva Mozes Kor, and your own next crucial insight, is that through the magic power of forgiveness you can attain total freedom from the past.

By rising above the great pain of having been hurt and in being the injured party, you free yourself entirely from the memory and its emotional impact. You relinquish any imprint left behind by the experience and energetically disengage from the perpetrator, the so-called victimizer. Many people try to find release from past experiences that haunt them, but as long as they hold on to their position as victim, finding a final release is practically impossible. People in their 50s, 60s, and 70s can still be tearful, brood, and feel hurt when recalling certain events and people from their early childhood. They live so much in the past that they seem to be capable of carrying this pain with them even to the grave. Forgiveness is the *only* way to halt the chain reaction of the past and to be free in the now.

This is a subtle, energetic principle: by holding a grudge, we remain tied to the victimizer. In this respect, love and hate are very similar—both are strong emotions that have the power to make a binding connection between our energy field and that of another person. It is ironic that we eventually live with those we resent so much for the rest of our lives.

The process of forgiveness involves two stages that I call "cut and include." First, you cut the bond with your victimizer. By letting them go, you actually let yourself go. We often think that our forgiveness is for others, but in reality it is primarily for us. We should understand that our forgiveness does not free the other person from responsibility; rather, it frees us from our imagined responsibility for the other and the other's fate. We are not the judges of that person, and so, when we do judge, we only sentence ourselves to a life of imprisonment—to forever remaining caged within the memory and occupying the position of the victim.

Once you have cut the unhealthy bond, your heart expands to such a degree that it has plenty of room for the other person as well as the past event. From this generous standpoint, you include and assimilate the other in your heart. The implication is that you no longer have an enemy. The enemy existed only when you were small.

Your heart loves forgiving. The reason it loves forgiving is not only moral—morality belongs to the mind. It is because it recognizes that as soon as it activates this magic, you have the chance to be liberated in a way that not even a heartfelt expression of regret on the part of the other person could achieve. This profound letting go fills you with so much joy that after experiencing a first release, you will want to use this magical anti-memory power again and again.

Yet there is one more reason for the heart's love of forgiveness. When you let go of the expectation and the false power of revenge, you are able to love the other to such a degree that you also become fully capable of loving yourself. Forgiveness releases your divine essence and the recognition of your own beauty and purity. While an unforgiving bitterness is deeply unsettling, the state of forgiveness reflects the greatest, most lovable part of yourself.

Don't say it is impossible for you to forgive because your case is especially painful. Always bear those instances in mind of other people, people just like you and me, who have forgiven far worse wrongdoings. If Eva Mozes Kor could look a Nazi in the eye and give them amnesty, you could do the same with your parents, partners, and other, more insignificant enemies.

Always remember that by forgiving them, you give yourself a chance to start a truly new life. If you want to be able to open up to your current and future relationships, you should understand that you cannot do this if you avoid the act of forgiving. The suspicion and fear of pain that were

imprinted in you then would continue to follow you, hindering your capacity to love and trust. On the other hand, if you are able to forgive someone wholly and sincerely, you will no longer fear disappointment since you know that you will be able to forgive again; you have unleashed this heart's power in you forever. And so, to be fully in the present, allow your heart to erase your past.

Exercise: Forgive actively

Return to the list of ten disappointing experiences from the previous exercise and use it to make a list of all the people toward whom you hold a grudge or feelings of disappointment. If a few more instances or people come to your mind now, add them to the list.

Even if you think you have already forgiven them, more or less, or that you have had the chance to go some way toward forgiving them in the course of a therapeutic process, this time use this opportunity to forgive them from the bottom of your heart. Inspired by the insight that forgiveness is the power that sets you free, let them go—and in doing so, let yourself go.

Do not forgive them reluctantly, but with joy. Let your heart surround them with love. Whether it is "fair" or not is not important. In the game of life, the question of who was right is unhelpful and often also unknowable. What really matters is whether *you* are free here and now and whether you are paving a new path for yourself to tread.

You can do this by writing a loving letter to each person, or at least to the most important people to you on your list. You don't need to actually send your letter, since this is not about them but about you. If you wish to undergo an even more profound release, ask someone you trust to represent your victimizer in an exercise. Ask them to sit in front of you with their eyes closed and for 15 to 30 minutes treat them as if they really were that person. Speak to them without interruption. It is absolutely fine for you also to share with them in the process your resentment and difficulty to forgive. This is also a part of such a heart expansion. Who knows, perhaps your partner in the exercise will be inspired too and ask you to help in their own process of self-release.

You will know that you have succeeded when you think of the person who hurt or disappointed you and experience no contraction in your heart. If you are able to say, "I have nothing in my heart toward this person besides love," it means you are free.

Fourth Secret:
The Ability to Love

Your heart doesn't need a process to be able to love

"Before I'm able to give something to others, I need to heal and to receive enough love myself"—how many times have I heard this statement uttered by people who are preoccupied with self-development! However, as logical as it may sound, this principle of first-receiving-then-giving is actually one of the greatest myths of the heart.

Once again, it is the mind that convinces us that in order to be in a position in which we are able to love and to give, we first need to undergo a long and intense process of healing and rehabilitation. Before we exhaust our own limited reserves in order to give to others, we must feel good enough ourselves. We need to receive love, in order to learn to give love to ourselves and to heal deep-seated traumas and emotional wounds. We have the general feeling that "one day we will be ready to love"—but not yet, not today.

By now, you will have almost certainly spotted the deceit: it is a strategy of postponement caused by the fear of being the one who gives everything but eventually is left with nothing. Since you are so desperately deprived yourself, the mind argues, it is not fair that you should give to others when you yourself don't receive enough.

Your mind is very calculating. It treats your emotional reserves of love and giving as if they were savings kept hidden in a bank, while approaching others with a begging bowl, as if it were poor. When you do as your mind bids, your heart always feels empty, and your need to be healed and to be given love feels like a bottomless pit.

Of course, there is always some truth in what the mind says. It is fairly obvious that the "human" part of our heart, the part that has acquired some difficult memories along the way, needs some rehabilitation and nurturing. A healing process is essential to enable us to eventually achieve emotional maturity. To be able to communicate with others in a solid and stable way, we must feel independent and complete within ourselves.

Yet even if we are in need of such release from the past and emotional maturity, we should not feel restricted or hampered in our capacity to fulfill love. The renowned saint Mother Teresa is an inspirational example. This woman, who despite all the controversy surrounding her was one of the most generous people in history, actually felt unrecognized and unheard by God in her own spiritual life. Her letters, published after her death, convey a deep frustration that no matter how much she gave, she met only silence, emptiness, and darkness inside. [5] At the same time, she proclaimed with confidence, "Intense love does not measure, it just gives." [6] Although some part of her was still emotionally wounded, she was entirely able to express love and to realize love. It is clear that Mother Teresa knew this most astonishing secret power of the heart: an ability to love and to give at any time, without the need to first prepare or achieve growth ourselves.

*

There is a part of our heart that is ready at any moment for the act of love. This means that your heart can open here and now. You just have to allow this part of it to awaken in you.

We are all familiar with this concept. Any new parent knows that they can always find a place in their heart for their crying baby, even when they are on the verge of collapse physically. Any therapist would confirm that even when their own life is full of crisis and conflict, as soon as they are with a patient, they miraculously manage to regroup their own emotional forces. In times of difficulty and distress, complete strangers can find enough compassion and courage in their hearts to help one another—even if they haven't undergone any psychological healing process.

One sunny day, I was walking with friends and family in a forest. My daughter, who was seven years old at the time, was running and jumping ahead of us with one of her closest friends, who was two years younger. At a certain point they paused, hesitating in front of some shadowy pathway, which, through their inexperienced eyes, seemed enchanted and even creepy. The younger girl said to my daughter, "There is no way I'm entering this pathway." Though my daughter was clearly terrified too, she suddenly drew strength from some unknown part of herself, assumed responsibility for the hazardous journey and, taking the other girl's hand firmly, responded, "Don't worry. I will take care of you."

The heart is like an emergency storehouse, where all the qualities that your mind seems to lack are kept, for when it needs them the most: courage, faith, conviction, and, above all, generosity. That's why, even if you feel like a lost child yourself, you are able right now to shelter, protect, and nourish someone else in need.

Exercise: Finding abundance within your heart

Think of someone you are able to love and serve right now—regardless of your current circumstance. It could be your child or dog, partner or parent, a dear friend or a patient, someone you admire or even some divine being, such as Jesus.

Close your eyes and access as intensely as possible your capacity to love and serve. Feel how your heart grows warmer and fuller. Visualize the person to feel how your heart opens up effortlessly to them.

After a few minutes, when this feeling is filling you completely, stop visualizing the other person and concentrate on the feeling only. Allow it grow and expand, until it permeates your entire body and being.

Now, ask the feeling to lead you to its origin; it is your link to your heart's abundance. Simply follow the feeling all the way to its origin until you manage to tap into these natural reserves. It may feel like a cool pool of sweetness and goodness, or a burning fire of love. Immerse yourself in this refreshing spring or empowering energy field for around 5 minutes. Then, slowly and gently, open your eyes.

This is not a mere "exercise." It is more a reminder that at this very moment, your heart knows how to love. You simply allow this special part of your heart—which has no need to be healed since it has never been broken or wounded—to express itself. This is the essential quality of our heart, its true nature.

We need to understand that the heart *is* abundance, but people often experience the very opposite—an empty feeling at the center of their chest, as if it were hollow. This feeling is not the true state of the heart, but rather a detachment from it, caused by the decision to erect a wall around and enclose the heart. If you access the heart behind the wall, you will find it overflowing, eager to love and to give.

As long as we believe that, in terms of our emotions, our heart needs to feel fulfilled and appreciated for it to become "full," we will have this strange hollow feeling in the chest.

In reality, the heart is never really dependent and is not in a "state of waiting," since it is by nature a *source*. A constant and uninterrupted stream of deep emotions flows out from the heart—ironically, the very same emotions that everyone hopes to receive from their environment.

This energy field beating within your chest is the source of what I call "non-causal emotions." Ordinarily, our emotions are experienced in response to events and people. If, for example, someone shows us affection, our heart seems to "open up"—or, more accurately, our mind agrees to momentarily uncover the forever-open heart. As far as our heart is concerned, it is a self-generating emotional flow. It is already full of sweetness and warmth, beauty and love, meaning and contentment.

In Plato's "Symposium," the comic playwright Aristophanes gives a speech on love, describing his own mythology of how man was at first a complex being, with two faces, four hands, and four legs. Since man was too powerful, Zeus decided to cut him in half, thus creating men and women who constantly crave to return to their original union. Their essential experience is of being "halved." [7] Even though this description is amusing and resonates with the sense of lack and longing that many experience, the heart is never "halved."

It is complete, and connected within itself, producing from within everything needed to "feed" the emotions.

The mind is driven by an inherent and unfulfilled sense of lack. Unlike the overly cautious mind with its give-and-receive calculations, the heart is calm and restful, aware of its own considerable worth. We all intuitively associate "generosity" with the heart, yet we tend to believe that this is something that should be gradually developed rather than the heart's very nature.

Do you know any stories of people who had nothing or very little and yet were still incredibly generous? Despite what your mind would have you believe, generosity has nothing to do with possessions, since it is in your heart regardless of what you may stand to gain or lose. Once we realize that there is never a good excuse for not loving at any given moment, we begin to comprehend this incredible truth: our heart is open even when it feels closed. We recognize this whenever we are in conflict or have a strained relationship with someone and choose to close our heart—deep down we know we could open up if we only wanted to. We hear a whisper in our ear. Yet sometimes we simply don't want to pay attention to it, because then we would "lose" the argument. However, ours is the only loss—missing out on one more opportunity to love.

Recognizing that the heart is not a needy and hungry focus of the emotions but rather a complete entity will enable you to finally let go of the calculating aspect of your approach to relationships. You can calmly draw on some of your hidden

reserves of love and begin to share them generously. This is
an inner law: the more you give, the more this natural abundance will be revealed and activated.

*

If there is any *real* path to emotional maturity, surely it lies in gradually agreeing to access this part of our heart, without fearing that if we let love flow, our story as beings with a *need* for love might come to an end.

In a way, it is true that we need love—yet not so much to receive it as much more to give it; to know for sure we have it inside us in abundance; to sense it as a part of ourselves. After all, the heart experiences fullness not when it receives but when it finally gives everything stored inside it waiting to be used.

We are all thirsty for the presence of love in our lives—for a good reason. Yet our calculating mind tells us that the only way to achieve this is by expecting and demanding more love. This is how we stray from seeing the heart as a natural reserve of love and confusingly translate the intense and burning wish for love into the need to be loved. If we're honest enough, we will sooner or later admit that this need could never be fulfilled because it is a false need. Even when we do receive love, we still feel dissatisfied and even more insecure. If someone were to be generous enough to tell you one hundred times a day "I love you," you would find that you still feel "hungry," since that is not the "food" that feeds our soul.

The heart's real nourishment is to give. It loves to give, because it is a center of dedication and devotion. That is why even if you undergo a very intensive emotional therapy, in the end it will throw you back to this reality of the heart, here and now.

Exercise:
Activating the heart's abundance every day

Whenever you feel your heart is "closed," get in touch with this inner wealth. Pause and visualize your open and exposed heart beating behind the wall. This can help you recognize just how abundant it is and how much it wants to love. If you feel you cannot possibly love at a particular time, try to make a conscious choice to act out of this abundance of love inside you. Make sure that the palm of your right, giving hand remains soft and relaxed to maintain an energy flow of sharing. You can even willingly "lose" in arguments by letting this generosity "win" sometimes.

Even if you feel you are in great need of self-healing, be sure not to block the flow from the heart. Give a little every day—a flower, a poem, some generous and encouraging feedback—and you will soon realize that this can sometimes be a stronger healing factor in your process.

If you're feeling courageous, try for a limited time—such as for a week or a month—to focus only on giving. Then see what happens: aside from your mind's warning signals, did you really miss out on anything? Did your heart truly lack anything?

When you feel the need to be loved, appreciated, or recognized, write it down and then translate your need into what you could give in this situation. For example, "I need to be recognized" can become "I want to recognize others more" or "I want to be recognized by the abundance I spread in the world around me."

If you do all this, you will soon experience feelings of happiness, as you have found the key to the secret that your heart has been trying to tell you all along: it was ready to love even when you believed it wasn't.

Fifth Secret:
Emotional Transformation

Your heart has the powerful ability to transform any internal energy

As a spiritual teacher who has had the privilege of helping thousands on their journeys of personal growth, I have persistently encountered one of the biggest problems involved with inner transformation today: the huge gap between how much we understand mentally and our emotional reality.

While our mental development has reached an impressive level of sophistication and many people are able to gain profound insights, their basic emotions remain unchanged. The result is that people understand how they "should" react and behave, but when primal emotions take over, they are at a loss to find a way out. Everyone knows that they should not be jealous, yet sometimes they can't help it when jealousy grips their heart. So they feel trapped, "watching" with their minds the emotional turbulence taking place in the heart.

Sometimes an in-depth therapy is able to bring our emotional center into alignment with our much clearer minds. However, this seems only to be effective with certain emotions and emotional patterns, while others remain stubbornly unaffected and may plague us for many, many years. The truth is, we can't really tell why some emotional patterns are so resistant to change.

In the absence of any real solution for this painful discrepancy, the only way your mind can cope is by that old yet efficient strategy, "suppression": overruling the emotional center through intellectual understanding. We simply use self-analysis as a weapon against these strong emotions, while suppressing all disturbing feelings to avoid ever having to acknowledge them again.

To help us get along well enough in life, suppression is very good at its job. A cognitive understanding of what is happening within us does help us to better control ourselves. But in the long run, the emotions we have hoped to bury become more twisted and complicated. Often, they transform into illnesses, or into forms of addiction and obsession.

The reason your mind is so bewildered and powerless in the face of such emotions is that it doesn't speak their language. Emotions speak a language so primal and instinctive that our rational thinking simply cannot learn or understand it. Energies such as desires, fears, and tensions—many of which we need to face on a daily basis—strike the mind as too vague and elusive to comprehend. For this reason, the very idea of real emotional transformation can often seem incomprehensible: does that actually mean to live one day without all those unfathomable yet so familiar feelings that seem closer to us than our own breath?

As with many of the heart's secret powers, only a few people know this: that the greatest transformer of the human system is the heart.

*

Your heart acts like a powerful magnet. It has the tendency to attract any emotion or feeling, including desires, tensions, or fears. It does so easily, and you will soon understand why.

To activate the heart magnet, you must change the location of your "presence" from your head to your chest. As soon as you relocate your center of gravity to your chest, all energies are drawn to it and are soon absorbed by it.

An energy sucked into the heart cannot escape its immense cauldron. It soon melts away, changing its nature radically. In this context, the heart is like a digestive system of the emotions, taking in substances and extracting their nourishing elements and subsequently expelling the remaining parts that are not needed.

Exercise: Activate the general magnetic force of your heart

Just as you did in the "Basic Heart Activation," feel and visualize how your entire focus and sense of self are gently sinking from the area of the head to the chest. Feel that your chest has become your center of gravity, where you find yourself and where you get in touch with the world. Imagine that the chest has become your new head, as if now it had its own eyes and ears. Let the head area become as transparent and spacious as possible. Feel that in a way you no longer have a head on your shoulders but, rather, an empty space. Let the heart at the center of the chest become "heavier," assuming the role of the center of your body and the bearer of your upper parts.

Imagining that the chest has its own eyes and ears, ask yourself, "How does it look at everything? What does it see?" and "How does it listen to everything? What does it hear?"

As you settle in your heart, feel it as it begins to awaken to its role. Feel its strong pull, which can act like a magnet for all possible energies. Realize that it quickly starts magnetizing energies from both above and below (the head and gut area in particular). Perhaps you can already notice that the heart is naturally attracting these energies—indeed, it is very difficult to experience any contradictory element when your heart has become the center of your being.

Most spiritual transformation practices deal with the raising up of lower energies all the way to the head—where the dormant "third eye" and "crown chakra" reside. Raising your energy to the head could certainly work if you wish to transform inner forces and impulses into abstract and expanded spiritual states.

An interesting example is the Tantra system, both Taoist Tantra and Yogic Tantra, which includes practices that transform sexual energy and sexual pleasure into mental and spiritual energies. Practitioners of the system learn how to activate their sexual parts and to then conduct their awakening force through their subtle channels all the way to the tip of their head.

Though great Tantric masters have also been aware of this secret of the heart, they have made use of it to transform sexual energy only rarely. As a powerful magnetic force, the heart can more easily and quickly transmute our sexuality. The heart is closer than the head to the pelvis, in both simple physical and emotional terms: unlike our mental world, the language of the emotions is not so different from the language of impulse and passion. In addition, the heart transforms our desire into a far more active and engaged energy of higher emotions, such as love and compassion, and heals and deepens our relationship with our partners.

This is done in a very simple way. While desire initially awakens within the sexual system, in order to transform it into a more refined type of energy, you need to first settle in the chest area. Unlike the shifting downward from the head toward the heart, in this case the movement is upward from the pelvic area toward the chest. From here it is quite an easy matter to draw out the sexual energy, absorb it, and to eventually direct it toward the outer world. In this way, desire turns into love.

⋆

But how is it that the heart holds within it such a tremendous transformative power? What makes it so magnetic to all energies within us? The answer is simple: love. Everybody intuitively knows this—that in the whole world there is no stronger energy than love. No other force can resist its power.

And so, when love is present, any lower and weaker energy submits to it, since all energies yearn and long for love.

This is a delicate point: just as all of us long for love, so too any other energy or force in us seeks it. Desires and addictions, for example, are like deep hunger and thirst that can never be satisfied. People yearn for a state that could satiate their hunger and thirst, not knowing that they indirectly strive for the experience of love.

In truth, at the deepest level most of the conflicted dynamics within our mental and emotional worlds are the outcome of our loss of contact with the power of love. As soon as our heart is empty, the human system becomes disoriented and lost, leaving space for more primitive thoughts and emotions to take hold, such as desire, anger, jealousy, fear, and resistance. Think of your emotional system as a motherless child. Wandering alone in the world, it goes astray.

Our heart knows that only love can satisfy the soul and fulfill deep emotional hunger and thirst. Without love, everything is disoriented, but when love returns, it halts the flow of wrongly directed energies. All emotions are immediately drawn to it and are happily absorbed in it. Love returns everything to its original state.

*

Your heart's immense power of love transforms base emotions and feelings, thanks to one special capacity: its ability to include and contain all and everything.

The heart is a natural repository. It effortlessly holds within it all that it encounters. In fact, it is so all-encompassing that it doesn't even need to alter any energy, emotion, or feeling that is held within it. That is why "acceptance" is intuitively associated with the heart. When you are so all-encompassing, you do not have to wage war against things.

This gives the heart a great advantage over the mind. The rational mind is in a state of constant conflict since it can never contain, only contradict. When it cannot overpower some emotion or feeling directly, its solution is suppression. The heart, on the other hand, has no need to battle with any force. With its all-encompassing nature, its method of over-coming is sweet and tender. The heart instantly envelops

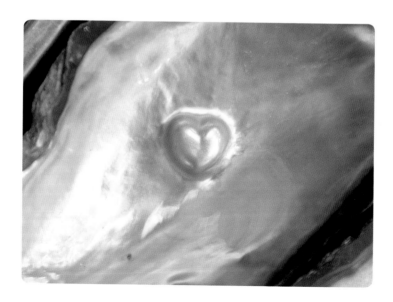

the emotion, surrounding it with wholesome positivity, and cleanses it from any distorted egoistic tendency. Eventually, it elevates the emotion to the higher domain of selflessness and goodness. Most of all, it reminds every part of us what it loves more than anything else and where it is most natural to reside.

Needless to say, since the heart has no need to reject any energy, when you center yourself in your heart you no longer need to suppress emotions.

We all know the magic effect that a kind word or warm hug can have—how all tension melts away in an instant. We mistakenly believe that we need to be given this word or hug from the outside, but this power to melt away all tension is within our heart at this very moment.

The heart can have this effect on any emotion or feeling in us, including anger, desire, or fear. It is like a parent responding to everything that our inner child expresses. It acts not out of the desire to get rid of something, but simply to soothe and fill with goodness and kindness.

With such a sense of overwhelming goodness, directed toward both ourselves and others, we cannot mistreat our own being or the beings of others. Observing and communicating with the world inside and outside us, we quickly realize how impossible it is to remain narrow and selfish from this new position of our being. This is why when you center yourself in the heart it is very difficult to maintain self-destructive addictions and obsessions.

*

Being able to place yourself in the heart to enable it to have this great transforming action is very simple. Whenever you encounter some tense or intense energy inside you, physically shift your center of gravity to the middle of the chest.

Although it seems quite reasonable to center yourself in your head, since this is the location of cognition and perception, in reality it is a space in which we feel quite uncomfortable. That is why our shoulders and neck often feel burdened. Our heads too often feel overloaded, tense, and aching. On the other hand, at times of desire or anger, when we act entirely impulsively and are out of control, we may feel that our center has moved to the pelvic region or to the belly.

In both cases, it is wise to shift our center to our heart. In physical terms, the heart is located in a particularly spacious area, far more spacious than the rather small head. The entire expanse of the chest can easily accommodate unbalanced energies from both above and below and transform them.

As soon as you sense the unbalanced energies appearing in you, move your center to the chest area. The more you settle there, the easier it will be for your heart to act with its full magnetic force. To start with, if you are unable to fully move to the chest area, you may find that it helps to visualize sending the emotion or feeling to the heart as in an elevator: imagine that feelings from below the heart, such as from the pelvis or the gut, are on the second or third floors and you're moving them up to the fourth; thoughts from above, which are on the fifth or sixth floor, take the elevator down to the fourth too—the button you press to call the elevator to go up or down is in the chest.

Alternatively, imagine that while firmly centered in the heart, you are drawing up the energy, either from below or from above, as if sucking it through a straw. The wonderful thing is that you don't need to actively push the energy upward or downward; you draw the energy from the area of the heart. If you have settled well enough in your heart, you will realize that it quite naturally attracts the energy you wish to transform.

Exercise: Transform any energy now

Think of a certain emotion or feeling, thought, or desire with which you have been struggling for a long time. If you cannot summon one up too clearly at the moment, try bringing to mind an image of a situation that provokes such an emotion. This will soon arouse any accompanying feelings and sensations.

As soon as you are experiencing these feelings and sensations intensely, bring your center to settle as firmly as possible in the chest. Feel the energy from your new position in the chest and draw it to the heart. Don't try to force this energy; allow it to be drawn into the heart, naturally and effortlessly.

Let the heart contain, digest, and transform this energy. Explore the way it changes within the heart. Give it the time to melt away and turn into a different quality or feeling.

Turn this energy outward, as if it were an arrow that is pointing toward the outside world.

Examine how you perceive the feeling or emotion in its previous, untransformed state. Can you still experience these feelings or emotions with the same original intensity? Ask yourself also how you could act now with this transformed feeling.

Try to follow this process as often as possible. Letting the heart consume any negative or limiting energy and transforming it into the invincible power of love is not only emotionally rewarding but also a condition of significantly improved well-being.

You can apply this process to transform sexual energy during lovemaking. You will avoid having to learn complicated techniques and it will change your love life for the better. Simply center in the heart whenever sexual arousal occurs.

You can also do this with difficult situations such as stage fright, an argument, or stress at work.

A similar process of transformation can be applied when facing difficult external energies like negative emotions or angry opinions. Simply settle in the heart, contain and transform the energy, and keep the heart's direction outward, streaming the renewed energy outside you. Remember the secret of the open heart: so long as your heart is flowing outward, it cannot receive external energy and therefore can never be damaged.

Sixth Secret:
Empowerment without Limits

Your heart can be your source of strongest motivation

Look at this question and think how you would answer it honestly: What is the source of energy, the impetus, and motivation for everything you do in life?

Some people never consider this and remain unconscious of what drives them to do what they do. However, this question is immensely important, since whatever drives you dramatically changes the way you experience your actions and their results. If, for example, every day you go to work simply to earn money, your experience of it will be quite superficial and functional. If you do something only because you have to, out of duty and obligation, you will often pause to wonder why on earth you are doing it.

Generally speaking, many people derive their energy from ambition and will. They want to achieve something, or have a number of goals, and their will drives them to wake up in the morning to a brand-new day. There is no doubt that, together, ambition and will are a mighty source that has clearly powered tremendous individual and collective processes in the world. These energies can even provide enough stimulation for you to be eager to get to work or to immerse yourself in work to the extent that you work longer than the normal hours. Indeed, the desire for recognition, success, achieving powerful social status, or earning a lot of money can be highly stimulating. Yet too often, because such ambitions are equated socially with being "driven," those who do not naturally share them feel unable to play the game.

Many millions of people don't seem to share these personality traits and as a result assume they are unfit for the competitive arena. They simply distance themselves from it and leave it to the more aggressive and ambitious. This illustrates a deep-seated belief—that we have to choose between the two extremes of either wanting power and success at the expense of stress and struggle or letting go and being satisfied with a narrow life and an unambitious attitude. In light of this conviction, when allowed to go unchecked, most people measure their sense of self-worth according to their degree of "confidence" or "no-confidence" in the game of life.

There is an inherent problem with ambition that the ambitious sometimes sense and the non-ambitious intuit. This kind of motivational force is extremely limiting: it exists without necessarily being tied into any deep sense of *meaning*. This is why a highly motivated individual is capable of waking up one morning, after many years of tireless engagement with the world, feeling completely worn out and wondering: "What is the point of all this? Why am I constantly chasing after such things?" Indeed, ambition and will do have a downside and ironically, considering the intensity they provoke in us, they often lead to a sense of emptiness.

Even with strong ambition, there is no real "why." You do something because you think you want to reach something or somewhere, yet you don't exactly know why you should do so. A significant number among our capitalistic, money-oriented, and competitively driven humanity behave exactly like this—rushing constantly and frantically to achieve without having even one good and clear reason. The side effect of this empty ambition is a deep frustration, which is usually resolved by seeking yet more destinations and goals.

I once spoke to a highly active and relatively successful cinema actor. He admitted quite frankly that no matter how much success he achieved, he was still always thinking of how much he hadn't accomplished and so ultimately remained frustrated. The truth is that frustration is like the opposite side of the coin to ambition: if you're ambitious, you're frustrated. Why? Because there are always higher mountains to conquer and people who have managed to conquer them. Even highly successful people look at even more successful people with envy and feel disappointed in themselves.

*

What, therefore, could be our source of true and healthy motivation?

As always, when we think of potential sources of energy and power, our mind rarely suggests looking to our heart. It may instead include more obvious sources such as physical energy, excitement, desire, craving, emotional recognition from others, and, of course, the desire for security—and will probably overlook love, at least as a driving force or a source of motivation.

To your mind, the heart seems, if anything, like the calming aspect of life where you cherish those dear to you, along with special times and experiences of tenderness and intimacy. The heart is where you get to relax in between or following achievements. The heart seems so far removed from the competitive arena that no one in their right mind could imagine it as a highly engaged participant and co-creator in this world of tensions.

As always, this would seem to make sense because your mind knows little about the heart's secret powers, including that the heart has an unstoppable drive.

The heart can animate us not only in what we feel but also in what we do. It holds the power to enable us to achieve all our authentic goals. And it is entirely capable of facing all the pressures caused by the effort and struggle that we undergo as we make our way in the world. In some cases, it actually exceeds willpower in its capacity to withstand pressures and hardships. Its secret is simple: when you have a really good reason for what you do—a genuine "why"—you are naturally willing to go to great lengths to realize your goal.

Perhaps this is what the German philosopher Friedrich Nietzsche meant when he wrote:

"He who has a why to live for can bear almost any how."

*

Love—the heart's only reason to relate to everything—is a source of endless empowerment. It is a power that can move mountains, and not just some tender and vulnerable feeling inside us.

Our history is filled with stories of real people, just like you and me, who were inspired to do tremendous things out of the sheer force of love: from Florence Nightingale to Etty Hillesum to Desmond Doss to Mahatma Gandhi to Martin Luther King Jr. If you are unfamiliar with some of them, please take the time to read their compelling life stories—learning about such figures can empower you to activate your heart as a driving force in your life too. Love and faith endowed them with unbelievable courage. It made them immune to fear of danger and death. They never used force, because they were equipped with only one weapon and one special armor. We remember them just as we remember those who were driven mainly by ambition. Yet we are also often very touched by those who acted out of love. This is because our heart recognizes them as its heroes.

This is why love can be a good enough and strong enough reason to wake up in the morning. I wake up in the morning because I love; what makes me rise from bed and enter a new day of action is love. I work out of love and meet people because I love.

At this very moment, I am writing this little book out of love. I could write it because I strive for a certain status, or because I wish to reach as many people as possible. I could write it driven by the wish to gain your recognition, or to convince and convert you. I could even write simply because I feel like writing.

Yet I am writing right now because I love.

I love writing; I love spiritual wisdom that can truly liberate; I love serving other people with clarity and empowerment; I love to focus on the secret powers of the heart, and the heart in general. I also, simply, love love.

If Gandhi could change the world driven by love, and for the very same reason I am able to write books, everyone else can find this force within themselves too. Try to define love as the reason to act or to do something yourself. It doesn't have to be something important. It could be the simplest, most mundane action. Think and feel: "I am doing this because I love"—and see what happens.

Exercise: Giving reason to everything you do

Gradually turn love into your one and only "why," your reason for doing anything. Start with the most basic action: as soon as you wake up in bed, say to yourself, even aloud: "I am waking up this morning because of love." Visualize love as if it were a silent engine, a powerhouse, behind your awakening being. Make this statement before any action: "I am now going to wash dishes out of love," or "I am walking my dog out of love," or "I am reading a book because I love."

Simply direct love toward that action, even if you don't believe in it at first. Cloak your action with love. Slowly you will see for yourself that it is a very valid reason, while at first even simply making the statement will change the way you experience the action. If the "magic powder" you have sprinkled with your words dissolves in the midst of the action, repeat the statement once again.

Follow this simple exercise and you will soon realize that your very experience of life is changing radically. This is because you have now put your heart into it. Indeed, that's the true meaning of "attention"—when you direct your heart toward something and envelop it with its unique type of awareness.

While the inevitable side effect of ambition is frustration, love goes hand in hand with a profound and wonderful experience of meaning, regardless of the type of action and its consequences.

When we activate love as a driving force, it's as if we have hit a hidden button that directly connects us to the meaning of life. Of course, no one really *knows* what the meaning of life is, or if there is one at all. Intellectually and even spiritually, we have absolutely no idea why we are here. Yet emotionally, we are able to have a feeling about it and to also actively communicate with it.

Interestingly, when our actions are packed with the fragrance of love, we no longer ask what the meaning of life is, since we have united with it. When we do everything we do out of love, our world is instantly filled with sense, value, and beauty.

In Spike Jonze's masterful movie, *Adaptation* (2002), Donald Kaufman confides to his twin brother, Charlie, one of his biggest secret decisions in life. Charlie recalls that there was a time in high school when he was observing Donald from the library window talking to a classmate named Sarah Marsh. In love with Sarah, he was flirting with her, and she appeared to be really sweet to him. But, Charlie discloses with embarrassment that when Donald walked away she started making fun of him with another classmate. Donald's response surprises his brother: he knew that, he says, he could hear them. "So how come you looked so happy," Charlie wondered. "I loved Sarah, Charles," Donald answered. "It was mine, that love. I owned it. Even Sarah didn't have the right to take it away. I can love whoever I want. You are what you love, not what loves you. That's what I decided a long time ago." [8]

Charlie Kaufman got it right: his love was undefeatable. Driven by love, you can never go wrong. Unlike other driving forces, love can never become corrupted or doubted, and it never has any side effects, like anger or frustration. You are untouched by comparison, since at the end of the day your only measure is how much love was in your heart when you did what you did—not how much you affected others and how successful you became. Even if in the eyes of society you "failed" completely, you would still know within your heart that, in reality, you didn't fail at all.

As a part of the heart's knowing, it is fully endowed with a direct *feeling* of what really matters in life. That is why it recognizes love as the one and only authentic driving force. But there is an even deeper source for this heart's knowing.

The meaning of life is what we call the "first cause": what drove the universe to emerge from "nothing." We could never ask ourselves "why" this happened—even if there were some transcendent, divine answer, we would not be able to apply it to our logical reasoning. That's why we have a heart with its unique knowing capacity—it taps into that primordial reason, since it is connected to the heart of all creation.

Just as we wake up after a deep sleep—during which we reside in the nothing—by feeling the urge to move and to act, so too the divine mysteriously experienced this urge to bring forth something out of nothing. Why did the divine bring forth something out of "nothing"? This urge is translated in human language as "love."

We *are*, in so many ways, the embodiment of this urge. Our breath is made of it; our life force is made of it. Since you were made by love, your very cells respond to it and to its energy. For this reason, when you activate love as your driving force, your whole being at its deepest core feels that this is "right." The urge to act, create, and accomplish our acts of creation is derived from that divine memory of the "first cause" in us.

In fact, if you're not cynical or holding back while reading these lines, you are surely already responding to this with one big "Yes!"

*

More often than not, our actions feel devoid of meaning and everything seems tedious and dull. However, when love is behind each and every action, even the most ordinary activity acquires color, a new significance, since we have come into contact with the only reason that could instantly justify all our actions in the past, present, and future.

There is no action or activity in the world that cannot be redirected through the motivation of love, including what we call "work." "Work" is a very bad word to describe what we do most of the day. If this is what you do—"work"—how could you ever be happy? Even if what we do is out of necessity rewarded by money, we should still focus on either the aspect of "service" or the aspect of "creativity."

Say to yourself instead, "Now I am going to create" or "I am going to serve others"—whichever works best for you. Doesn't it radically change your experience of what you do? Virtually all work includes a service to others or some level of creativity. So transform your relationship with your money-making activity, work, career—first of all, by dropping forever the concept of "work," and second, by adding to it your ultimate "why?": "I am going to serve/create out of love." This could give a new meaning to the concept "labor of love."

That said, your particular form of paid service or creativity may differ from your deepest passion in life—and that is perfectly fine. Not everyone is able to combine the two, partly for the simple reason that not everyone's passion can be realized through goals and creative projects.

"Passion" is a strong word associated with heart motivation. Passion is a tremendous energy, yet one that is driven by a genuine love of a particular form of action. You can be passionate without even a trace of ambition. This can easily be seen in the pure enthusiasm of small children, yet it often gets lost and is buried deeply in most adults who are overcome by "duty" and activities driven by results. However, some do inspiringly retain this quality. Socrates, for instance, was passionate about philosophy until his very last breath, which is exactly what the word "philosophy" is all about—the love of wisdom.

Since the heart is a center of passion and devotion—devotion to whatever fills us with passion—look for the things that evoke passion in you and that you wish to devote yourself to. It doesn't have to be a particular career—it's fine to be passionate about relationships, animals, or photography as a hobby. While you fulfill your service to others out of love, you also need to define your true passion, or passions, and to declare your devotion to them.

Before you say, "I don't have any passions; I'm not so special," remember that next to our ambitions, desires, and obligations, we are all equipped with certain passions. They are the mark of the creative drive of the universe itself in us. If anything, ambitions are usually the false yearnings we have, longings we have "borrowed" from the people around us, but passions are completely original—as Donald Kaufman says, you own them.

Exercise: Define your heart's passion

Close your eyes, focus on your heart, and ask it: "What am I really passionate about?" Now listen—what does your heart tell you is your passion in this life? Forget ideas of career, success, or recognition. What would you do simply because you have a burning passion for it in your heart? What would you still do even if you were neither paid nor recognized for it?

Let the answer materialize slowly. Don't rush it, even if it requires a few days or even weeks. As soon as you recognize your passion, realize that you also came to the world equipped with the energy you need to follow it all the way. If your answer is exactly what you do for a living right now, consider yourself lucky, since you happen to be following the old adage: "Find something you love to do, and you'll never have to work a day in your life." [9] However, if your current occupation doesn't match up with the answer, ask yourself, "How can I ensure that my true passion does not get lost in the stream of my daily activities?"

Seventh Secret: Loving Yourself

Your heart sees your perfection even when you're imperfect

In 1990, American author and Buddhist meditation teacher Sharon Salzberg traveled to Dharamsala, India, for a Mind and Life conference with the Dalai Lama. The conference comprised a small gathering of psychologists, scientists, and meditators who were exploring the topic of emotional healing. When it was her turn to bring up a topic for discussion, eager to explore the suffering she had observed in both her students and herself, Salzberg asked the Dalai Lama, "What do you think about self-hatred?"

She describes how the room went quiet with anticipation. It was intriguing to notice the Dalai Lama's startled response. He turned to his translator, asking pointedly in Tibetan again and again for an explanation. Finally, when he looked at her once more, he tilted his head with eyes narrowed in confusion. "Self-hatred?" he repeated in English. "What is that?"

Salzberg goes on to describe that during the remainder of the session, the Dalai Lama repeatedly attempted to explore the nature of self-hatred with them. He found it very strange and groped for explanations. "Is it some kind of nervous disorder?" he asked, and then, "Are people like that very violent?" Baffled, he claimed, "But you have Buddha nature. How could you think of yourself that way?" [10]

While Eastern philosophy may have no concept of self-hatred and self-condemnation, many people in Western culture feel incapable of fully accepting themselves. Consciously or unconsciously, we are in a state of conflict with who we are: with the body we "received," with the past we were compelled to experience, with our built-in limitations and stubborn patterns of behavior, with everything that we will never manage to be as well as with the specific challenges of our lives.

This is why we could hardly imagine perceiving ourselves— just as we are at this very moment—as divine, whole, and complete. We believe that the experience of perfection is a future achievement that we would perhaps be worthy of once we had justified it sufficiently through achievements, strict self-correction, and recognition. In our subconscious, we think that one day, we will be able to deserve our very own self-love.

Interestingly enough, countering this inner discontentment with spiritual knowledge of our "Buddha nature," or "divine nature," doesn't seem to heal the wound either. I have met numerous spiritually engaged people who, despite all their spiritual experiences and insights, were still struggling with feelings of unworthiness and self-judgment.

The reason for this is simple: your mind can never allow self-acceptance, since it is by nature self-contradictory and divisive. In fact, thinking is wholly based on a duality that prevents you from ever relaxing into yourself.

Consider this sentence carefully: "*I* cannot accept *myself.*"

Your thinking has created two beings: "You" and "Yourself." Obviously, since you are not two but only one, one of the two—either "You" or "Yourself"—does not really exist. The one that doesn't exist is the "I" at the beginning of the sentence. Now, who is this "I" that finds it so hard to accept "itself"—your authentic and most natural self?

This unreal "I" is the part of your mind that is borrowed from society. It is a voice that thrives on many internalized voices, which you have picked up along the way from parents, the authorities, classmates, colleagues, TV, commercials, and collective concepts of a very specific culture. This "I" consists of comparisons made by others, which have resulted in comparisons you have started making with others.

Because of these internalized voices, your mind is split. When these voices tell you that you are not good enough, you constantly make the mistake of identifying with them and calling them "me." This is how you eventually arrive at the awkward feeling of "I dislike myself." In reality, any feelings you may have of being an unworthy, sinful, or "bad" person are not really yours.

The social "I" keeps whispering in your ear what you "should" be like. It always suggests an alternative, better reality of yourself, whether it is a future version or an unrealistic one. This other reality is a fantasy and cannot be fulfilled. We could never be "enough" for the fantasy. As a result, we are unable to like ourselves as we are—not as long as the "I" rules and "myself" is constantly denied.

Ironically, this "I" that seems to keep encouraging "itself" to be better hinders your true self from flowering. The mind achieves very little through self-condemnation. Try to think of a time when self-condemnation worked for you and made you succeed in what you did. Can't think of such an event? That's because there can be no such thing. No flower ever emerged from the soil as a result of self-judgment. Flowers only grow because it is natural to do so.

In reality, only "myself" exists. Therefore, to be able to relax into ourselves we need to dissolve this "I." However, our mind could never do that. Remember that contradiction and opposites are part of its very nature. This is why as long as we listen to the mind, we are doomed to live with this strange struggle of the self against itself.

Exercise: Face and unveil your inner critic

This exercise involves writing. Create two columns: one headed "I am" and the other "I should be." Start writing down all your self-criticisms, entering them in both columns. For example:

I am not ambitious enough | I should be more ambitious

Write down as many self-criticisms as possible, at least ten. When you have finished, consider each statement in the right column very carefully and, being honest and looking into your heart, ask yourself: "Should I really? Is it true?" Also ask yourself, "Who in me says 'I should be'? Who is this 'I'? Who told me that? Where did I get it from?" You could even alter the statements by changing the beginning to: "The false social 'I' tells me that … I should be more ambitious."

Slowly reveal the truth behind the "should." This may be painful and may even evoke some resistance in you. Your false "I" would probably tell you, "But this is true! You really should be that!" At least while carrying out the exercise, don't listen to it and keep on questioning.

You will notice that each sentence in the right column ends, directly or even indirectly, with "not enough": "I am not beautiful enough," or "I am not courageous enough." Go one step further by revealing the source of the statement: a comparison to someone else. For instance, "I am not successful like…" Take a look at all the other people

that your false "I" tells you that you should resemble. Isn't it
odd that you're meant to be all those people? Is it true that
you should be like any of them? Who would live your life,
then, if even you became someone else?

While revealing the external voices and observing the way
the social "I" invalidates your being, move your attention to
the heart in the way you did in the "Basic Heart Activation"
and get in touch with "yourself" within the heart. Feel the
steadiness and silent confidence of "yourself," even in the
face of such harsh judgments.

Your mind could never allow profound self-acceptance because it is divided. Your heart, on the other hand, is complete and whole by nature. In your heart, there is only one you. It is filled with this intimate sense of "myself," since the heart is where your true self—the nature-given or God-given self, exactly as it was meant to be—resides.

This authentic self-recognition is not as abstract as your "Buddha nature," which means that somewhere, beneath your human imperfections and flaws, there lies a transcendent, perfect nature. It is really a recognition of your design as a whole. Your entire humanness, with all its beauty and shortcomings, is embraced, since the heart does not need to wait until you become perfected, or to look beyond your imperfections. It requires no recognitions and successes to justify such an acceptance and doesn't even seek a heavenly reassurance that it is indeed the time. It sees you as a complete being right here, right now.

This is the seventh secret power of the heart: it can reveal wholeness, even now when we are full of flaws and weaknesses; even when we feel ourselves most damaged, unworthy, and undeserving. This is because it is connected at this very moment to the sense of our inherent divinity—the one we achieved already at the moment of our birth.

Unlike the mind, which always argues with our natural design, the heart knows that each of us is one of nature's patterns, a unique design that is both wonderful and flawed. It easily recognizes that this, too, is "perfect" in its own way. While the mind strives for perfection, the heart sees wholeness as perfection: zebras could never be elephants, and volcanoes could never be "like" rivers. Zebras can only be what they are, which is of course limited and beautiful at the same time. In precisely the same way, you are "limited" too: some things you can do, and some things you simply can't. But do you expect elephants to hover over flowers like butterflies? If not, why do you expect yourself to do things you are simply unable to do?

From this healthy perspective, the endless attempts of your thoughts to mend something that has never been broken seem ridiculous. Your nature-given unique design is both incomparable and self-justified. The cosmos itself, with all

its genius and grandeur, produced and permitted it. If anything, your design is God's problem, not yours. Whoever complains about it could be directed to the all-organizing intelligence of the universe itself.

Do you honestly think that you were created on the wrong day in heaven? Do you imagine that in heaven's human factory, you were produced by one sloppy angel who woke up that morning in a particularly bad mood?

Not accepting ourselves implies rejecting the universe as a whole. Why are we so ready to acknowledge that the universe is complete and perfect, that each and every lizard and caterpillar is complete and perfect, while we miraculously are the only element that deviates from the holy pattern—only we, specifically, are some kind of a cosmic error? How could this even be? Everyone in their right mind would agree that life is a miracle. Doesn't that mean that you are a miracle too?

Write an imaginary letter to God or to the cosmos, and try your utmost to convince it why only in your case, it made a mistake. Then write a reply from God or the cosmos, explaining why it created you in this way and what exactly it wanted you to be. The result could be very revealing, as you realize that the universe wants you to be you.

*

Self-acceptance means accepting the cosmic will. After all, who we are is what the divine or the universe wanted us to be. If the divine will had been that we should be without any limitations, it would have taken care of that in the first place.

As far as the divine will is concerned—and unlike the way we think—we are at this very moment in the right place and in the right body, with the right limitations and the right obstacles in our path.

Our heart has no quarrel with our innate limitations and shortcomings. It clearly knows that all human weaknesses, difficulties, and obstacles *must* be there as a necessary balance for the divine powers in us and as a vital means for evolution and learning. In this sense, in our heart there is no doubt that this imperfection is also a type of perfection—one that could never be perceived by our thinking, which forever measures, evaluates, and compares, yet can be sensed through feeling and knowing.

This is the way the cosmos wants us to be—beautiful and weak, confused and brave. As soon as we accept that wholeheartedly, we discover a new type of beauty and perfection: not the perfection that is the opposite of limitation but one that also includes all possible limitations.

There is a deep spirituality behind self-acceptance. Indeed, when self-acceptance is very profound, it is not merely a psychological self-embrace but also a spiritual experience. It's a path to God and to cosmic wholeness. All we need to do is to pass through self-acceptance as if it were a gate leading us directly to the divine reality, since inner wholeness is our most immediate link to the greater wholeness.

Some people talk of "surrendering to the higher will." From the mind's perspective, this could easily strike the same old chord of becoming better and more worthy in the eyes of God. Yet true surrender starts with first accepting yourself just as you are.

*

Self-acceptance is a tremendous power of the heart. It puts an end to the social "I"; it pierces through all the layers of inauthentic self-image and shows you the wholeness of your reality, the "good" and the "bad" as one cosmic-given "you." Then it opens you up to love, to being able to also love others as perfect wholes. It connects you to the total feeling of the universe and enables the full flowering of all your gifts and abilities on the firm foundation of a deep positive sense of yourself.

Yet there is one more reason to consider the act of self-acceptance a great power of the heart. While too often it is perceived as a sort of "last resort" for the weak—hugging the "poor me"—it is actually the only genuine foundation for real confidence. Confidence can grow from self-love, since we no longer listen to social voices that weaken us and tell us how we should be. We are simply following the path that was set out for us by our very own cosmic-given pattern. We have no choice but to be ourselves, and since this self was designed by the greatest genius, we can also take pride in it.

Everyone knows Frank Sinatra's classic recording of "My Way." The song's lyrics are sometimes taken for granted as some obvious cliché. But could you write these words as if they were your own—declaring with self-honor and self-dignity that even your failures have been an expression of a singularly unique path? Be aware that such confident words could be written only by someone who had first accepted themselves. This is not arrogance—it is the healthiest feeling you could ever have.

In the end, you are doing your best following your own path; you can do no more and you can't really deviate from it and get lost. This is a law of natural design: we are all doing the best we can, within the limitations of our own inherent pattern. Can you honestly say that you're not doing the best you can?

Exercise: Being one with yourself

Let your center of gravity slowly move from the head to the chest area. Feel how by doing that you also move away from the duality and self-struggle of the mind to your already complete heart. Allow your heart to show you "yourself" now, just as it is, with its benefits and hindrances. Notice that while the mind overemphasizes the disadvantages, your heart has a straightforward and sober balanced vision of both.

Look at "yourself" from the heart. You could even visualize your physical self with your heart's "eyes." Observe yourself in this way, enjoying the way the heart regards without judgment and with complete forgiveness. Free yourself from the eyes of the world and, leaving all fantasies of "should be" behind, see yourself only through the eyes of the heart.

Now generously pour love into yourself. Activate the self-generating, non-causal emotional flow of the heart and turn it toward yourself. Pour into yourself all the warmth you have ever hoped to receive. Since the heart can hug you from within, gently embrace your natural design and nourish it with deep emotions and unconditional contentment.

Place your left, receiving hand on the lower center of your chest and place your right, giving hand over the left. Repeat the mantra "I am myself" for 10 to 20 minutes and let it resonate throughout your being from head to toe. This is your one true heart mantra, which holds the power to dissolve the "I" and to allow unity with yourself. Remember that you are not trying to create such unity; you are merely finally revealing it. Notice how your hands relax into the chest, enabling warmth to flow from your heart into your hands and the other way around.

Feel how as soon as you attain this instant inner wholeness, it also connects you to the outer wholeness. When you are yourself, everything else falls into place: the sky, the earth, all animals and people follow their natural design just like you in a cosmos that is always only one. When you cease excluding yourself from the cosmic pattern, all and everything becomes included within your heart. Allow this vision to take place, to immerse yourself even more in the cosmic ocean of wholeness. Just as you are, you are now a blessed pulsating particle of the universal being. When you accept yourself, you are home.

The "Heart Gym" Exercise

While we tend to think of the heart mainly in energetic and spiritual terms, it is also an "emotional muscle." It has a physiological aspect, including physical posture and position, which it is important to keep fit and flexible. The following self-guided meditation can help.

Basic instructions

Practicing the "Basic Heart Activation" and the "Heart Gym Exercise" on a regular basis, alternating them every day, may eventually lead to a constant opening of your heart—so that it opens and never closes again.

In this exercise, once you have read the instructions carefully, you may close your eyes or keep them open.

Step one: Open up your heart's wings

First, make sure that your chest does not sink onto the solar plexus, or diaphragm. We usually find that the chest is resting heavily on the diaphragm. Gently stretch and widen the diaphragm area, so that it becomes a firm platform that can support the chest with ease. In terms of chakras, this enables the unhindered flow from the third and highly individual chakra to the fourth and highly unitive heart chakra. Feel how you can breathe freely from the diaphragm to fill the chest with air.

As you allow this free passage of breath and energy, feel how the chest can widen. Feel how the shoulders are gently pulling apart from one another, as if you have wider shoulders. In this way, the chest can correctly be supported by the solar plexus and the shoulders can be supported by the chest.

Now, breathe into this whole area—solar plexus, chest, and shoulders—as one, making this part of your body rise and fall, rise and fall. Make sure that your back at the level of your chest also widens. Realize that your chest is much bigger than you have ever experienced before, almost like the wings of an eagle, so that with every in-breath you open up your wings and with every out-breath, you fold them again.

You could even visualize wings emerging from the center of your back, on a level with the base of the chest. This allows a deepening of your breathing. Follow this breathing and visualization with gentle movements of the shoulders and the upper back, particularly moving your shoulders backward and forward to open up your chest even more.

Step two: Flexing your heart's muscle

For this stage, close your heart completely, as if you are clenching a fist at the center of your chest. Don't create a painful feeling there, but just feel how you are suffocating and blocking the energy. Clench your heart tightly—closing it as much as possible, as if it were saying "I don't want to open up today." It may help to move the shoulders and bend forward in order to contract the center of the chest even more.

Bring your heart to the point where it feels utterly closed—and then, at once, open up. Just as you did before, breathe into the solar plexus, chest, and shoulders as one; open up your wings with every in-breath. Experience the release and comfort—how it feels so much better. Again, you can be helped with movement of the shoulders and the back. Feel how more energy is flowing as a result.

Now, once again clench the "heart muscle." Again, clench it tightly but not painfully; try as much as possible to close it and to make it sink inwardly. Think, "I don't want to open up," in the most childish and resistant way. "I don't want to open up to people, to situations, to the world…"

Take the clenching to the maximum—and then, relax. Feel how the energy flows much better and breathe into this unity of solar plexus, chest, and shoulders. Realize how unhealthy it is to close the heart.

For one last time, contract your chest. Think to yourself: "I don't want to let go of disappointments. I don't want to let go of my sadness, my grudge, my anger. I am keeping it all to myself. I am not going to ever trust." Close it, close it, close it…

Then, finally, relax. Feel how you breathe more fully. Let the energy flow. Make some slight movements with the shoulders—to allow the freed energy to flow from the solar plexus to the chest and upward to the throat, from where it is finally released. As an expression of this release, you may feel the need to yawn or sigh. This makes sense, since the throat is the gateway through which everything stored in our heart is released.

Return slowly from meditation.

Pay attention

Sometimes when we undergo the intense process of heart-opening, we experience the very opposite: pain and contraction in the chest, and a general feeling that there is not enough space in the heart. Don't allow yourself to lose faith. It is actually a good sign, an indication that you're stretching your "heart muscle" more and more.

We need to realize that this "muscle" may be so contracted that when we attempt to open our heart, we are met with an initial resistance. This resistance is not necessarily mental or emotional. It is simply the result of the ingrained habit of many years of keeping the heart small and hidden. You are now breaking through the wall, and this is what you feel shattering. As soon as the wall comes down, your heart will once more be the natural all-inclusive space it has been always and forever.

Love has come to rule and transform;
Stay awake, my heart, stay awake.

Rumi

Sources

1. Steven Novella, MD, Brain cells in the heart?, Neurologica Blog, 12.8.2013, https://theness.com/neurologicablog/index.php/brain-cells-in-the-heart/

2. Elizabeth Clare Prophet, The Buddhic Essence, page 115, Summit University Press, 2009

3. 30 Good Minutes, Eva Kor, Spiritual Journey – Forgiving our enemies, Youtube interview, 2013; https://www.youtube.com/watch?v=VxqQbXoDtIc

4. Batchelor Television, Eva Mozes Kor: A Story of Forgiveness, Youtube interview, 2010; https://www.youtube.com/watch?v=rwvbtuIz6Hs&t=24s

5. David Van Biema, Mother Teresa's Crisis of Faith, Time Magazine, 2007

6. Hemul Goel, 8 Quotes by Mother Teresa, India Today, 2016

7. Plato, Symposium, translated by Benjamin Jowett, Pearson, 1956; http://classics.mit.edu/Plato/symposium.html

8. Charlie Kaufman, Adaptation, Movie Script, 1999; http://www.dailyscript.com/scripts/adaptation.pdf

9. Garson O'Toole, Choose a job you love, Quote Investigator, 2014; https://quoteinvestigator.com/2014/09/02/job-love/

10. Sharon Salzberg, Buddha Nature, Rebel Buddha, 2011; http://www.rebelbuddha.com/2011/01/buddha-nature/

Shai Tubali, chakra expert, spiritual teacher, authority in the field of Kundalini and the subtle body system, lives in Berlin, where he runs a school for spiritual development and holds seminars, trainings, satsangs, and retreats. Since 2000 he has worked with people from around the world, accompanying them on their spiritual path. He has written 20 books on spirituality and self-development,  including *Good Morning, World*, a bestseller in Israel, and *The Seven Wisdoms of Life*, winner of the USA Best Books Award and finalist for the Book of the Year Award.

To access the Basic Heart Activation and Heart Gym exercises go to:

https://shaitubali.com/heartvideos

Stay tuned by subscribing to Shai's YouTube channel and enjoy access to a wealth of additional material on *Unlocking the 7 Secret Powers of the Heart.*

Other books by Shai Tubali:

The Seven Chakra Personality Types, Red Wheel/Conari Press (2018)

Indestructible You: Building a Self that Can't be Broken, Changemakers Books (2015)

A Guide to Bliss, MSI Press (2015)

The Journey to Inner Power, Changemakers Books (2015)

The Seven Wisdoms of Life, MSI Press (2013)

The Missing Revolution, Crusader eBooks (2013)

The Mystical Enlightenment Of Friedrich Nietzsche, Theophania Publishing (2013)

Picture credits

Powerful yet concise, this revolutionary guide summarizes the Hawaiian ritual of forgiveness and offers methods for immediately creating positive effects in everyday life. Ho'oponopono consists of four consequent magic sentences: "I am sorry. Please forgive me. I love you. Thank you." By addressing issues using these simple sentences we get to own our feelings, and accept unconditional love, so that unhealthy situations transform into favorable experiences.

Ulrich Emil Duprée
Ho'oponopono
The Hawaiian forgiveness ritual as the key to
your life's fulfilment
Paperback, full color throughout, 96 pages
ISBN 978-1-84409-597-1

Both Ho'oponopono, the Hawaiian forgiveness ritual, and family constellation therapy help to heal our relationships with the world around us and bring healing to our inner world. This hands-on book brings together what belongs together, providing beginners with an introduction and easy access to the subject and the more experienced with fresh insights.

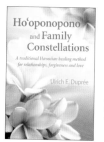

Ulrich Emil Duprée
Ho'oponopono and Family Constellations
A traditional Hawaiian healing method for
relationships, forgiveness, and love
Paperback, full color throughout, 160 pages
ISBN 978-1-84409-717-3

Discover everything you need to know about the luminous infinity symbol. Use the many simple exercises contained in this book for decision-making, improving your relationships, reconnecting the analytical and the emotional sides of your brain, and much more. The lemniscate can be used in a wide variety of ways.

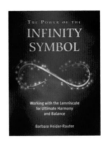

Barbara Heider-Rauter
The Power of the Infinity Symbol
Working with the lemniscate for ultimate har-
mony and balance
Paperback, full color throughout, 128 pages
ISBN 978-1-84409-752-4

Healing Crystals is a comprehensive and up-to-date directory of 555 healing gemstones, presented in a practical and handy pocket guide format. In the revised edition of his bestseller, Michael Gienger, famous for his pioneering work in the field of crystal healing, describes the characteristics and healing powers of each crystal in a clear, concise, and precise style, accompanied by four-color photographs.

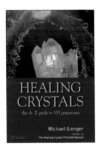

Michael Gienger
Healing Crystals
the A–Z guide to 555 gemstones, 2nd edition
Paperback, full color throughout, 128 pages
ISBN 978-1-84409-647-3

This pocket pharmacy of healing stones embraces many applications. Although describing only twelve stones, the breadth of its scope resembles a home pharmacy. From allergies to toothache, you will find the right stone for every application. This handy little book offers you the essence of our modern knowledge of healing stones.

Michael Gienger
Twelve Essential Healing Crystals
Your first aid manual for preventing and treating common ailments from allergies to toothache
Paperback, full color throughout, 64 pages
ISBN 978-1-84409-642-8

Tapping into children's seemingly inherent love of rocks and stones, this accessible introduction to gemology provides youngsters with a basic understanding of the properties that crystals possess, the power of color, and the metaphysical importance of positive thinking. Divided into seven sections, each chakra is explored and visualization exercises are included in order to experience the chakra's energy.

Margaret Ann Lembo
Color Your Life With Crystals
Your first guide to crystals, colors, and chakras
Paperback, full color throughout, 112 pages
ISBN 978-1-84409-605-3

This is an easy-to-use A to Z guide for treating many common ailments and illnesses with the help of crystal therapy. It includes a comprehensive color appendix with photographs and short descriptions of each gemstone recommended.

Michael Gienger
The Healing Crystal First Aid Manual
A practical A to Z of common ailments
and illnesses and how they can be best treated
with crystal therapy
Paperback, with 16 color plates, 288 pages
ISBN 978-1-84409-084-6

Gem water can be a valuable aid to health, providing effective remedies and acting quickly on a physical level. Water is known to carry mineral information, so by placing crystals in water it becomes charged with the crystals' energy. Drinking gem water as a therapeutic treatment is similar and complementary to wearing crystals, although the effects are not necessarily the same.

Gem Water should be prepared and used with care; this book explains everything you need to know to get started.

Michael Gienger, Joachim Goebel
Gem Water
How to prepare and use more than
130 crystal waters for therapeutic treatments
Paperback, full color throughout, 96 pages
ISBN 978-1-84409-131-7

For further information and to request a book catalog contact:
Inner Traditions, One Park Street, Rochester, Vermont 05767

Earthdancer Books is an Inner Traditions imprint.
Phone: +1-800-246-8648, customerservice@innertraditions.com
www.earthdancerbooks.com • www.innertraditions.com

EARTHDANCER

AN INNER TRADITIONS IMPRINT